Tell Me Where It Hurts

Paul Groves

Stanley Thornes (Publishers) Ltd

Contents

The Operation ———————————————————— 3
3 parts: Doctor, Nurse, Patient

The Hospital Visit ——————————————————— 14
2 parts: Patient, Visitor

Doctor! Doctor! ———————————————————— 23
2 – 5 parts: Doctor, Nurse, Patients

© Paul Groves 1980

All rights reserved. No part of this publication may be reproduced or transmitted in any form or by any means, electronic or mechanical, including photocopy, recording, or any information storage and retrieval system, without permission in writing from the publisher or under licence from the Copyright Licensing Agency Limited. Further details of such licences (for reprographic reproduction) may be obtained from the Copyright Licensing Agency Limited, of 90 Tottenham Court Road, London W1P 9HE.

Originally published in 1980 by Hutchinson Education

Reprinted in 1990 by
Stanley Thornes (Publishers) Ltd
Ellenborough House
Wellington Street
CHELTENHAM GL50 1YW

98 99 00 / 20 19 18 17 16 15 14 13

British Library Cataloguing in Publication Data

Groves, Paul
   Tell me where it hurts.—(Spirals)
   1. Readers
   I. Title   II. Series
   428.6'2   PB1126.D4

ISBN 0 7487 0251 2

Cover illustrations by Simon Rees, cover design by Ned Hoste
Set in IBM Pyramid
Printed and bound in Great Britain at Martin's The Printers, Berwick.

The Operation

3 parts: *Doctor, Nurse, Patient*

Scene: The operating theatre of a hospital. A nurse enters with a patient on a trolley.

Doctor	Wheel him in, nurse.
Nurse	There we are, sir.
Doctor	Ah, good afternoon, Smith.
Patient	Jones, doctor.
Doctor	Jones?
Nurse	Yes, it's Mr Jones, doctor.
Doctor	I thought Smith was coming in first.
Nurse	No, this is Jones.
Doctor	Oh, I was expecting Smith.
Nurse	Well, it says Jones.
Patient	I'm Jones.
Doctor	All right, my good man.
Nurse	It says Jones on the name tab, doctor.
Doctor	But I've got the notes for Smith.
Patient	Look, I'm Jones!

Doctor   All right, my good man.

Nurse   Yes, it is Mr Jones.

Doctor   Ah well, I suppose one will do as well as another. Right, Mr Smith.

Patient   Jones!

Doctor   Yes, I know, Jones. Now where do you feel sore?

Patient   I don't feel sore.

Doctor   You must feel sore.

Patient   I don't.

Doctor   Well, where is the pain then?

Patient   In my foot.

Doctor   In your foot. Now don't play jokes on me, my good man.

Patient   It is my foot!

Doctor   Poor chap. He's all mixed up. He doesn't know what he's saying. Now, nurse, pull back the sheet. I want to see his tummy.

Nurse   Yes, doctor.

Patient   My tummy!

Doctor   Yes, your tummy. I'm going to take your appendix out.

Patient My appendix!

Doctor Yes, your appendix. Just lie down and let's get on with it.

Patient But it's my toe!

Doctor Now look here, Smith.

Patient Jones.

Doctor I know when an appendix should come out.

Patient But it's my big toe.

Doctor But I've got the X-rays here. Look, Smith, that's what's wrong.

Nurse But this is Jones, doctor.

Doctor Of course, yes, Jones.

Nurse It's his left toe.

Doctor Are you sure your appendix is OK?

Patient Yes, it's fine.

Doctor Well, I might do both at the same time. Save you coming in again. Now, your left toe.

Nurse The *left* toe, doctor.

Doctor Yes, I know, the left toe.

Patient That's my right toe.

Doctor	Keep calm, my good man. Here is my left hand and here is your left toe.
Patient	That's my right.
Nurse	You are facing him, doctor.
Doctor	How do you mean?
Nurse	Well, when you are facing him your left hand is by his right toe.
Doctor	Is it?
Nurse	If I turn you round you can see.
Doctor	Well, so it is. We live and learn.
Nurse	I've found the notes, doctor.
Doctor	Your toe, right.
Patient	No, left.
Doctor	Don't start that again. Blast, now I've dropped the notes.
Nurse	I'll pick them up. Oh dear, they have fallen in this pool of blood.
Patient	Oh.
Doctor	Hold them for me, nurse. I can't hold a thing this morning. What a night I had last night.
Nurse	Did you, doctor?

Doctor   Oh, I put a lot away!

Nurse   Yes, doctor.

Doctor   Now just look at my hands. Couldn't take the top off my egg this morning. Ha! Ha! My wife had to do it for me.

Nurse   Yes, doctor.

Doctor   Right, your toe. This one?

Patient   No, the big one.

Doctor   They all look alike to me.

Nurse   Shall I tie a bit of string on it?

Doctor   That's a good idea. I know what it is. I haven't got my glasses on.

Nurse   They're in your top pocket, doctor.

Doctor   Where?

Nurse   The left one.

Doctor   Oh, the left one. Perhaps I'd better tie a bit of string on that as well, ha! ha! Blast!

Nurse   What is it?

Doctor   These aren't my glasses. They belong to my wife. Never mind. I suppose they'll do.

Patient   Oh.

Doctor   Lie down, please. Right, let's start. Knife.

Nurse   Knife.

Doctor   Fork.

Nurse   Fork?

Doctor   Salt and pepper.

Patient   Salt and pepper?

Doctor   I'm sorry, I'm hungry. I've had no dinner. Couldn't keep a thing down this morning. Now I'm a bit peckish. You haven't got a bag of crisps on you? Salt and vinegar?

Patient   No, I haven't. Let me out of here.

Doctor   Now don't panic, Smith.

Patient   Jones.

Doctor   Jones. I can see you're upset. Most people get upset at a time like this. It may help if you shut your eyes and cross your fingers. I always do.

Patient   Oh!

Doctor   Right. What did I do with the knife? We'll soon have that toe off.

Patient   But it hasn't got to come off.

Doctor   Hasn't it?

Nurse   The notes, doctor.

Doctor   Ah yes, the notes. No, I can't read them.

Nurse   You've got them upside down.

Doctor Ah, so I have. What does it say, nurse? I can't see with all this blood on the paper.

Nurse   It says, straighten out the toe, sir.

Doctor Ah yes, straighten out the right toe.

Patient The left toe.

Doctor When I say straighten out the right toe, I mean the right toe.

Patient The left.

Doctor I mean the right toe and not the wrong one.

Patient Oh.

Doctor The left toe is the right one and the right one is the wrong one.

Patient Yes.

Doctor Right. Now, where's the one with the string on? Ah yes, knife.

Nurse   Knife, doctor.

Patient Just a minute.

Doctor What is it now?

Patient Aren't you going to put me out?

Doctor But you've only just come in.

Patient I want to be put out!

Doctor Do you want to go to the toilet?

Patient No, I want to be put to sleep!

Doctor Oh, that. Yes, we'd better do that. Where's the chap who does that, nurse?

Nurse He's gone down the bookie's.

Doctor The bookie's!

Nurse Yes, the bookie's.

Doctor What a cheek!

Nurse Yes, doctor.

Doctor What a cheek to walk out of this hospital!

Nurse Yes, doctor.

Doctor What a cheek to walk out of this hospital and go to the bookie's and not take my bet with him. Now I shall have to phone.

Nurse Yes, doctor.

Doctor The phone, nurse.

Patient Doctor....

Doctor Shall I put a bet on for you? No, it might not be worth it.

Nurse I've got the number. The phone's ringing. What shall I say to the bookie?

Doctor	Tell him I want five pounds each way on Bleeding Foot and Sudden Death.
Patient	Oh no!
Doctor	I always bet on hunches.
Patient	Oh no.
Doctor	Put on the TV, nurse.
Nurse	The TV, doctor?
Doctor	The first race is due.
Patient	But. . . .
Doctor	Don't worry, I'll wake you up if it gets exciting.
Patient	Oh!
Doctor	Now, where did I put my fags?
Nurse	I don't know, doctor.
Doctor	I had them when I was cutting open the last patient.
Nurse	Yes, you did, doctor.
Doctor	I didn't sew them up inside, did I?
Nurse	Well, they were on his tummy when I last saw them.
Doctor	Better get him back in here.

Nurse   Yes, doctor.

Doctor I mean, there were six fags left in that packet. I can't afford to lose them.

Nurse   Yes, doctor.

Doctor Now, the hammer.

Patient The hammer?

Doctor To send you to sleep until that chap comes back from the bookie's.

Patient I'm getting out of here. [*He runs away*]

Doctor Come back, Smith.

Nurse   Come back, Mr Jones.

Doctor Get him back at once, nurse.

Nurse   [*Returning*] He's gone, doctor.

Doctor It was all because he was getting it free. In the good old days a patient had to pay up and shut up. There was no messing about.

Nurse   But Mr Jones was a private patient, doctor.

Doctor A private patient?

Nurse   He was paying.

Doctor Get him back at once!

Nurse   Yes, doctor.

Doctor Tell him I'll do both feet for the price of one.

Nurse Yes, doctor.

Doctor Tell him I'll do it cut price.

Nurse Yes, doctor.

Doctor Tell him I'll cut my price to the bone!
[*She runs off*]

The Hospital Visit

2 parts: *Patient* and *Visitor*

Scene: A hospital ward.   A patient is in bed with the curtains drawn round.   A visitor peeps in.

Visitor   How are you, then?

Patient   Eh?

Visitor   How are you, then?

Patient   Who is it?

Visitor   It's me.   Mrs Green.

Patient   Who?

Visitor   Mrs Green from next door.   You must be in a bad way if you don't remember me.

Patient   Oh, Mrs Green.

Visitor   Yes.   How are you then?

Patient   Well, I don't know really.

Visitor   It's a good thing I've come then.   I can cheer you up.

Patient   Thank you very much.   I could do with that.

Visitor   I've got some grapes for you.

Patient   I like grapes.

Visitor   But I sat on them in the bus.

Patient   Oh.

Visitor   But there are a few left. And you could suck the skins of the rest.

Patient   I'll enjoy them later.

Visitor   Yes, I said to my Fred, I'll go and cheer Ben up. I mean, you had a very nasty smash.

Patient   Did I?

Visitor   Don't you remember?

Patient   No.

Visitor   Your brain must be in a bad state.

Patient   My brain?

Visitor   Yes. You may never be the same again. Still, let's look on the bright side. Your memory might come back in a few years.

Patient   Years?

Visitor   It's just as well you can't remember the crash. It would only upset you if you started thinking about that shop.

Patient   What shop?

Visitor The shop you crashed into. It's a real mess. It's going to cost £1000 pounds to put it right.

Patient Oh no.

Visitor Can you remember your car?

Patient Let me see. It was new. It was red. Yes. Yes, I remember!

Visitor Well, forget it. You won't be seeing it again.

Patient My car. My lovely car.

Visitor You must keep looking on the bright side. The man at the scrap yard was glad to have the bits.

Patient Oh!

Visitor It's a good thing I came to cheer you up. You don't look too good, I must say.

Patient Don't I?

Visitor Very pale.

Patient Pale?

Visitor Just like my Aunt Lil before she died.

Patient Well, I don't feel too bad.

Visitor It's not how you feel, it's how you look. You don't mind if I have a grape, do you?

Patient No.

Visitor I mean, I've been visiting people in hospital for years and I can always tell when they're going.

Patient Going home?

Visitor No, passing over. To the other place.

Patient You don't mean I am, do you?

Visitor Oh no. You're going to be all right.

Patient Do you think so?

Visitor Yes. Yes. Anyway, if I thought you'd had it, I wouldn't tell you, would I? I wouldn't upset you by saying a thing like that. You don't mind if I have a grape, do you?

Patient No.

Visitor I don't expect you can eat them with all those bandages.

Patient Bandages?

Visitor Yes, I can't see much of you. You're bandaged from head to foot.

Patient I didn't know. I thought there were just these round my face.

Visitor Well, you'd get a shock if you saw yourself. You make me think of that film.

Patient   What film?

Visitor   'The Mummy from the Grave'.

Patient   Oh.

Visitor   I hope they know what they're doing.

Patient   Why do you say that?

Visitor   My Uncle Ted went in for his tonsils and they cut off his leg.

Patient   Oh.

Visitor   Is that blood?

Patient   Blood? Am I bleeding?

Visitor   No. I mean the blood in that bottle with the tube going into your arm. I'd keep an eye on that, if I were you.

Patient   Why?

Visitor   Well, my Uncle Ted had a bottle like that and someone put red ink in it.

Patient   What happened?

Visitor   That was the end of Uncle Ted. Can I have another grape?

Patient   Yes.

Visitor   A good job I came to cheer you up. You must have been really fed up before I came.

	I bet you were longing for someone to talk to.
Patient	I was asleep.
Visitor	Oh, these hospital chairs. Do you mind if I sit on the bed?
Patient	No.
Visitor	I've been on my feet all day.
Patient	Ow!
Visitor	What is it?
Patient	Ow!
Visitor	Do you want a nurse?
Patient	My leg!
Visitor	Your leg?
Patient	You're sitting on my leg.
Visitor	I'm sorry. I thought you had both legs in the air.
Patient	No, I've one in bed.
Visitor	I don't think it can do a leg much good being that high, do you?
Patient	Why?
Visitor	I mean, the blood can't get to it.

Patient Can't it?

Visitor My second cousin Dick had that trouble. His went green. They had to saw it off. Can I have a grape?

Patient Oh dear.

Visitor Shall I let it down a bit?

Patient No!

Visitor Just a little bit.

Patient No, please, leave it alone.

Visitor Please yourself, but it could make all the difference between on or off.

Patient On or off?

Visitor Oh, look at this chart at the end of the bed.

Patient I don't understand them.

Visitor It's all right if all those lines are low, oh dear . . . .

Patient What is it?

Visitor Let's talk about something else. After all, I have come to cheer you up. As your wife couldn't come . . . .

Patient Yes, where is my wife?

Visitor	Oh, she couldn't come as it was her night for having her hair done.
Patient	Having her hair done?
Visitor	Well, you don't want her to let herself go, just because you're in here on the ....
Patient	On the what?
Visitor	On the danger ... on the bed, I mean, on the bed.
Patient	Well, what about my son?
Visitor	Haven't you heard?
Patient	Heard what?
Visitor	About your son. It happened the day you had your crash.
Patient	What happened? What happened?
Visitor	Well I went in to tell him the news.
Patient	What news?
Visitor	About you. About the crash. Well, someone had to tell him. So I popped into your house and there he was up a ladder.
Patient	My son was up a ladder?
Visitor	Yes, he was just putting a picture on the wall. Well, I told him but he didn't hear me.

Patient   Has he gone deaf?

Visitor   Oh no. It was the drill.

Patient   What drill?

Visitor   He was drilling a hole in the wall to hang up the picture. Anyway, I went up the ladder, right behind him, and yelled in his ear.

Patient   Oh no. Oh no. Don't tell me.

Visitor   It's all right. Don't upset yourself. Your son is getting on very well. He'll be up and about in a few weeks.

Patient   Oh! [*He passes out*]

Visitor   Mr Wilkins, you have gone pale. Do you want a grape? There's one left. If you don't want to talk, just say so. [*The patient groans*] Oh, well, I can take a hint. I'll go now. Yes, I'll go and see your son. He's in the room next door. I'll pop in and cheer him up.

Doctor! Doctor!

2 – 5 parts: Doctor, Nurse, Patients

Scene: A doctor's surgery.
A patient in a cap enters rather nervously.

Patient   Doctor?

Doctor   Yes.

Patient   Doctor....

Doctor   What is it?

Patient   Well, I er....

Doctor   Yes.

Patient   Well, I er....

Doctor   Come on. Don't be shy.

Patient   I don't like to say.

Doctor   Come on. Get it off your chest.

Patient   You'll think I'm silly.

Doctor   No, I won't. I see lots of people. I am used to them telling me things. So come on.

Patient   I was all right when I got up.

Doctor   Yes.

Patient   But after I got dressed, suddenly ....

Doctor   Yes?

Patient   I got this ticking in the ears.

Doctor   A ticking in the ears?

Patient   Yes.

Doctor   You don't mean a buzzing sound?

Patient   No, it's a ticking.

Doctor   Loud?

Patient   Very loud.

Doctor   Tell me more about it.

Patient   Well, it's just tick tock, tick tock all the time.

Doctor   Oh!

Patient   And there's worse.

Doctor   Worse?

Patient   When I was coming here on the bus I heard bells.

Doctor   Bells!?

Patient   That's a sign of madness, isn't it?

Doctor   Well ....

Patient   I don't want to go mad. But this tick

	tock, tick tock is driving me crazy, and my head is feeling so heavy.
Doctor	Your head feels heavy, does it?
Patient	Yes. Oh dear. Please say I'm not going mad.
Doctor	Now calm yourself. You look perfectly normal to me. Let me start by examining your ears.
Patient	All right.
Doctor	Left okay. Right okay. Yes, your ears are clear.
Patient	Does that mean ....
Doctor	Just a minute, take off your cap.
Patient	Right, doctor.
Doctor	Give it here.
Patient	The ticking — it's much better. It's going away.
Doctor	And if I move over here, has it gone?
Patient	Yes, you're a marvel, doctor. You've cured me.
Doctor	Not only have I cured you but I can tell you where you left your cap last night.
Patient	Can you?

Doctor   On your bedside table.

Patient That's right. You're a marvel. How do you know that?

Doctor   Because you've got an alarm clock stuck inside your cap, you silly fool!

Patient Oh!

Doctor   Next please.

[A man comes in, bent in two]

Patient Doctor! Doctor!

Doctor   Well, come in.

Patient It's difficult for me to walk.

Doctor   I can see that. Come and sit down.

Patient I can't sit down.

Doctor   Well, come and stand over here.

Patient I'll try.

Doctor   How long have you been like this?

Patient I was all right when I went to bed.

Doctor   No pain?

Patient No pain.

Doctor   Yes, go on.

Patient   And then when I got up I was all right.

Doctor   Yes.

Patient   But I was just dressing when suddenly I couldn't stand up. I was bent over like this.

Doctor   Oh dear.

Patient   You must help me. I can't stand up. I can't sit down. I can't walk. I had to come here in a taxi.

Doctor   Let me take a look at you.

Patient   Right.

Doctor   Try to stand up a bit.

Patient   I can't. What's happened to me? Have I slipped a disc?

Doctor   I think I'll need a knife.

Patient   You're not going to operate here?

Doctor   Just a small cut.

Patient   Oh.

Doctor   There!

Patient   I can stand up. I'm better. What was it, doctor?

Doctor   You silly fool. Next time you're dressing don't button the middle button of your shirt into the top button hole of your trousers!

Patient   Oh!

Doctor   Good-bye. Next please!

[*A patient comes in sneezing*]

Patient   Doctor... atishoo. Doctor... atishoo.

Doctor   Don't tell me you've still got your cold.

Patient   Yes, doctor, and it's worse.

Doctor   But that's nearly two months now.

Patient   It still doesn't get better.

Doctor   Take off your shirt. I need to hear your chest.

Patient   Right.

Doctor   Yes, it's on your chest now. Have you been taking the pills?

Patient   Yes, every day without fail.

Doctor   Have you been out? A lot of cold winds this time of the year.

Patient   Atishoo! No, I sit all day by a warm fire.

Doctor   I don't understand it. Those are good pills. They always work.

Patient   Well, I take them.

Doctor   We need to go over this step by step. First of all, are you warm enough in bed?

Patient   Yes, I've got ten blankets.

Doctor   What about getting up?

Patient   I put on a warm dressing-gown.

Doctor   What about breakfast?

Patient   I have a good breakfast.

Doctor   What do you do then?

Patient   Then I get in a bath of cold water.

Doctor   You what?

Patient   Then I get in the bath of cold water.

Doctor   You get in a bath of cold water!?

Patient   Yes.

Doctor   Why?

Patient   You told me to. That's why.

Doctor   Rubbish. I didn't say that.

Patient   Yes you did – on the pills.

Doctor   On the pills?

Patient   Yes it says on the bottle: Take two in cold water three times a day.

Doctor And you've been getting into a cold bath three times a day?

Patient Yes.

Doctor You silly fool! It means put the pills in a glass of cold water.

Patient Oh. [*He goes*]

Doctor Nurse! Nurse!

Nurse Yes, doctor.

Doctor Are there many more out there?

Nurse Yes, doctor.

Doctor What a day! I've just had three fools in here. One had an alarm clock in his cap. The next one got his buttons mixed up. And the last one had been jumping into a bath of cold water every time he took a pill!

Nurse You must be feeling fed up.

Doctor I am. I wouldn't mind, but I'm not feeling well myself.

Nurse Oh, doctor.

Doctor Ever since I got up this morning I've had this tight feeling round my chest. I can't breathe properly. I've tried some pills but I still feel the same.

Nurse	Shall I get the other doctor?
Doctor	Yes, I think you had better.
Nurse	Just a minute, doctor. Take off your coat.
Doctor	Take off my coat?
Nurse	Yes.
Doctor	Can you see some spots or something?
Nurse	Not spots, but do you often wear a shirt with Mickey Mouse on it?
Doctor	Mickey Mouse?
Nurse	Yes, look.
Doctor	Oh no! I've got my little boy's shirt on. Ha! Ha!
Nurse	Ha! Ha!

The Spirals Series

Stories

Jim Alderson
Crash in the Jungle
The Witch Princess

Jan Carew
Death Comes to the Circus
Footprints in the Sand

Barbara Catchpole
Laura Called Nick

Susan Duberley
The Ring

Keith Fletcher and Susan Duberley
Nightmare lake

John Goodwin
Dead-end Job
Ghost Train

Paul Groves
Not that I'm Work-shy
The Third Climber

Anita Jackson
The Actor
The Austin Seven
Bennet Manor
Dreams
The Ear
A Game of Life or Death
No Rent to Pay

Paul Jennings
Eye of Evil
Maggot

Margaret Loxton
The Dark Shadow

Patrick Nobes
Ghost Writer

David Orme
City of the Roborgs
The Haunted Asteroids

Kevin Philbin
Summer of the Werewolf

Julie Taylor
Spiders

John Townsend
Back on the Prowl
Beware the Morris Minor
Fame and Fortune
Night Beast
SOS
A Minute to Kill

David Walke
Dollars in the Dust

Plays

Jan Carew
Computer Killer
No Entry
Time Loop

Julia Donaldson
Books and Crooks

John Godfrey
When I Count to Three

Nigel Grey
An Earwig in the Ear

Paul Groves
Tell Me Where it Hurts

Barbara Mitchelhill
Punchlines
The Ramsbottoms at Home

Madeline Sotheby
Hard Time at Batwing Hall

John Townsend
A Bit of a Shambles
Breaking the Ice
Cheer and Groan
Clogging the Works
Cowboys, Jelly and Custard
The End of the Line
Hanging by a Fred
The Lighthouse Keeper's Secret
Making a Splash
Murder at Muckleby Manor
Over and Out
Rocking the Boat
Spilling the Beans
Taking the Plunge

David Walke
The Bungle Gang Strike Again
The Good, the Bad and the Bungle
Package Holiday